Willhelm Shakespear, Bindery Hampstead

Songs From the Plays of Shakespeare

Willhelm Shakespear, Bindery Hampstead

Songs From the Plays of Shakespeare

ISBN/EAN: 9783337006860

Printed in Europe, USA, Canada, Australia, Japan

Cover: Foto ©Thomas Meinert / pixelio.de

SONGS . FROM THE . PLAYS OF . SHAKESPEARE

. ILLUSTRATED . BY PAUL . WOODROFFE

London: Printed for the Guild of Women-Binders . 61, Charing Cross Road . W.C. 1899

LIST OF ILLUSTRATIONS

ON THE SONGS FROM THE PLAYS OF SHAKESPEARE

ARIEL, who is the essential sprite of song, has often been attempted, if never entirely captured, in picture; and the same may be said of SHAKESPEARE'S SONGS. They lure every generation in turn to give them a pictorial and musical setting, after its own fashion. Fashions change; the charm of these SONGS, and their lyric fascination, are constant. The new presentment may not be, is very unlikely to be, the final and perfect one. It is pretty certain to be very unlike Shakespeare's idea, conceived in Elizabethan terms of music or colour, of his own SONGS set to a lyric or pictorial accompaniment.

Still, if it is good in its kind, the setting serves to make us turn to the original SONGS with a new sense of their delightfulness; and that is enough.

The wonderful thing about the SONGS is, that separated from their context in the plays—where their extreme felicity, dramatically considered, made one dwell mainly upon their stage merit—they should still strike one as so perfect in themselves. This sets aside the cavil of the Scottish critic who maintained that SHAKESPEARE'S SONGS would not bear mention in the same breath with Burns—save for the lustre of their dramatic framework. Better to consider how both wrote songs so inimitably, and both purely as song-writers, not as lyric poets in our later sense. As for Shakespeare, we may be sure that, though the names of his tunes are not given, he had a tune in his head for every song he wrote. The ballads heard at Stratford fairs, or the songs caught from the mouths of "the beggar-men of Chepe," or the folk-tunes sung by some Warwickshire Autolycus, served him well. Tunes like "Lady Greensleeves," "Crimson Velvet," "Light o' Love," "Three Merry Boys," and "The Bailiff's Daughter," and the familiar melodies of many a carol, and many an old country dance and fiddler's jig, waited to prompt his fancy at the exigent moment. The Duke in "Twelfth Night" may show you how good a prompter Shakespeare's memory was in these things, when he calls again for "the song we had last night," a song which happens to be one of the most tender and finely cadenced of them all, "Come away, come away, Death!" The little prelude and commentary the Duke offers upon it is in the true connoisseur's view, idiomatic as the lines that follow:

> "*Mark it, Cesario, it is old and plain:*
> *The spinsters and the knitters in the sun,*

And the free maids that weave their thread with bones,
Do use to chaunt it: it is silly sooth,
And dallies with the innocence of love
Like the old age."

Those plays in which Shakespeare makes the most use of the lyric leaven, using it not only for songs, but for passages of a sort of free recitative, or again of an unusual overflow of rhyme, such as "Love's Labour's Lost," "The Midsummer Night's Dream," and "The Tempest," are divided in point of time by such long intervals that the critic who would base any theory upon the chronology of the songs would be bold indeed. In any case, the reader here, looking at them through the agreeably uncritical medium of delightful illustration, would be likely to resent any attempt to bring the rules of the great Shakespearean critics into the question. Other poets than he, when the ebullience and heat of youth, and all its gay or sorrowful impulsiveness, were gone, may have lost their lyric grace and power. Shakespeare remembered his tune, whether of last night, or thirty years ago, and wrote his song, whether to fit the earthly humours of a grave-digger or the airy spirit of an Ariel, in just as well and beseeming a vein apparently at the last as at the first. The rhymer in him may a little have decayed ; the lyric poet and the song-writer never—so far at least as we can judge.

For Ariel, the last consummate creature of his lyric imagination, comes at the last. He is the spirit of all the airy harmonies and all the fugitive half-recollected tunes, one has ever heard or dreamt. Everything he utters has something of the inevitable lyric essence in it. "I drink the air before me" is his promise of good speed. The same sense of airy movement, and free passage, such as a song itself may win on the clear airs of sea-shore or hill-top, is in all his fluent exits and entrances; as where we find him described, when leading Ferdinand by the sea-shore, as "invisible, playing and singing." What elusive harp-strain, flying on from one ripple of silver strings to another, such as he may have heard from some Welsh triple-harp in the West Midlands, had Shakespeare in his mind as he wrote the lines that the scene ushers in?

"*Come unto these yellow sands,*
And then take hands:
* * * * *
Foot it featly here and there,
And sweet sprites the burden bear."

So far as the stage could possibly suggest such things, the appearance of Ferdinand, sitting and listening there, suggests the loneliest of lonely sea-places. But one hardly bears to read "The Tempest" as a stage-conditioned piece of art. It is a poem, that one recollects rather with the poetry that is, like the best of Shelley and Wordsworth, to be felt under quite another range of association than even the most ideal theatre can furnish. And so with Ferdinand's speech, sequent to the "Yellow Sands" melody :

> "*Where should this music be? i' the air or th' earth?*
> * * * * *
> *This music crept by me upon the waters,*
> *Allaying both their fury and my passion*
> *With its sweet air; thence I have followed it,*
> *Or it hath drawn me rather: but 'tis gone—*
> *No, it begins again.*"

Then come the famous "Full fathom five" lines—"the ditty" which, says Ferdinand so imaginatively, "does remember my drown'd father." In all this there is an art almost transcending art. It is like something struck out of nature, in a radiant, changing imagery. And it is the sense of such unforgettable melody, caught in a dramatic pause, like a fragrance of distant hay-fields caught at a town window by night, that makes these songs, like Ariel himself, so elusive—at once so tempting and so tantalising. Art, pictorial art or music, may succeed in interpreting them ; it is certain that criticism, however ardent, can do little with them.

ERNEST RHYS.

SONGS FROM THE PLAYS OF SHAKESPEARE

WHO is Silvia? what is She
That all our swains commend her?
Holy, fair and wise is she;
The heaven such grace did lend her
That she might admired be.

Is she kind as she is fair?
  For beauty lives with kindness:
Love doth to her eyes repair
  To help him of his blindness,
And, being help'd, inhabits there.

Then to Silvia let us sing
  That Silvia is excelling;
She excels each mortal thing
  Upon the dull earth dwelling:
To her let us garlands bring.

IT was a Lover and his Lass,
With a hey, and a ho, and a hey nonino,
That o'er the green corn-field did pass
In the spring time, the only pretty ring time,
When birds do sing, hey ding a ding, ding :
Sweet lovers love the spring.

Between the acres of the rye
These pretty country folks would lie.

This carol they began that hour,
How that a life was but a flower :

And therefore take the present time,
  With a hey, and a ho, and a hey nonino;
For love is crownéd with the prime
  In the spring time, the only pretty ring time,
When birds do sing, hey ding a ding, ding:
    Sweet lovers love the spring.

FIE on sinful fantasy!
Fie on lust and luxury!
Lust is but a bloody fire
Kindled with unchaste desire,
Fed in heart, whose flames aspire
As thoughts do blow them, higher and higher.
Pinch him, fairies, mutually;
Pinch him for his villany;
Pinch him, and burn him, and turn him about,
Till candles and starlight and moonshine be out.

SIGH no more, ladies, sigh no more,—
  Men were deceivers ever,
One foot in sea and one on shore,
  To one thing constant never :
—Then sigh not so, but let them go,
  And be you blithe and bonny,
Converting all your sounds of woe
  Into, Hey nonny, nonny.

Sing no more ditties, sing no mo,
  Of dumps so dull and heavy ;
The fraud of men was ever so
  Since summer first was leafy :
—Then sigh not so, but let them go,
  And be you blithe and bonny,
Converting all your sounds of woe
  Into, Hey nonny, nonny.

COME away, come away, Death,
And in sad cypress let me be laid;
Fly away, fly away, breath;
I am slain by a fair cruel maid.
My shroud of white, stuck all with yew,
O, prepare it!
My part of death, no one so true
Did share it.

Not a flower, not a flower sweet,
  On my black coffin let there be strown ;
Not a friend, not a friend greet
  My poor corpse, where my bones shall be thrown :
A thousand thousand sighs to save,
    Lay me, O, where
Sad true lover never find my grave,
    To weep there.

SWEET Flower, with flowers thy bridal bed I
strew,—
O woe! thy canopy is dust and stones;—
Which with sweet water nightly I will dew,
Or, wanting that, with tears distilled by moans:
The obsequies that I for thee will keep
Nightly shall be to strew thy grave and weep.

Pardon, Goddess of the night,
Those that slew thy virgin knight;
For the which, with songs of woe,
Round about her tomb they go.

Midnight, assist our moan;
Help us to sigh and groan,
Heavily, heavily:
Graves, yawn and yield your dead
Till death be utteréd,
Heavily, heavily.

FEAR no more the heat o' the sun
  Nor the furious winter's rages;
Thou thy worldly task hast done,
  Home art gone, and ta'en thy wages:
Golden lads and girls all must,
As chimney-sweepers, come to dust.

Fear no more the frown o' the great;
  Thou art past the tyrant's stroke;
Care no more to clothe and eat;
  To thee the reed is as the oak:
The sceptre, learning, physic, must
All follow this, and come to dust.

Fear no more the lightning-flash
  Nor the all-dreaded thunder-stone;
Fear not slander, censure rash;
  Thou hast finish'd joy and moan:
All lovers young, all lovers must
Consign to thee, and come to dust.

No exorciser harm thee!
Nor no witchcraft charm thee!
Ghost unlaid forbear thee!
Nothing ill come near thee!
Quiet consummation have;
And renownéd be thy grave!

I

WHERE the bee sucks, there suck I:
In a cowslip's bell I lie;
There I couch when owls do cry.
On the bat's back I do fly
After summer merrily.
Merrily, merrily shall I live now,
Under the blossom that hangs on the bough.

II

Come unto these yellow sands,
And then take hands:
Courtsied when you have, and kiss'd
The wild waves whist,

PW

Foot it featly here and there;
And, sweet Sprites, the burthen bear:
Hark, hark!
Bow-wow.
The watch-dogs bark:
Bow-wow.
Hark, hark! I hear
The strain of strutting chanticleer
Cry, Cock-a-diddle-dow.

III

Over hill, over dale,
Thorough bush, thorough brier,
Over park, over pale,
Thorough flood, thorough fire,

I do wander every where,
Swifter than the moon's sphere;
And I serve the fairy Queen,
To dew her orbs upon the green.
The cowslips tall her pensioners be:
In their gold coats spots you see,
Those be rubies, fairy favours,
In those freckles live their savours:
I must go seek some dewdrops here
And hang a pearl in every cowslip's ear.

NOW the hungry lion roars
  And the wolf behowls the moon,
Whilst the heavy ploughman snores,
  All with weary task fordone.
Now the wasted brands do glow,
  Whilst the screech-owl, screeching loud,
Puts the wretch that lies in woe
  In remembrance of a shroud.
Now it is the time of night
  That the graves all gaping wide,
Every one lets forth his sprite
  In the church-way paths to glide;

And we Fairies, that do run
By the triple Hecate's team
From the presence of the sun,
Following darkness like a dream,
Now are frolic: not a mouse
Shall disturb this hallow'd house:
I am sent with broom before,
To sweep the dust behind the door.

Through the house give glimmering light,
By the dead and drowsy fire:
Every elf and fairy sprite
Hop as light as bird from brier;

And this ditty, after me,
Sing, and dance it trippingly.

First, rehearse your song by rote,
To each word a warbling note:
Hand in hand, with fairy grace,
Will we sing, and bless this place.

Now, until the break of day,
Through this house each fairy stray.
To the best bride-bed will we,
Which by us shall blesséd be;

And the issue there create
Ever shall be fortunate!
So shall all the couples three
Ever true in loving be;
And the blots of Nature's hand
Shall not in their issue stand;
Never mole, hare-lip, nor scar,
Nor mark prodigious, such as are
Despiséd in nativity,
Shall upon their children be.
With this field-dew consecrate,
Every fairy take his gait:

And each several chamber bless,
Through this palace, with sweet peace;
And the owner of it blest
Ever shall in safety rest.

Trip away; make no stay;
Meet me all by break of day.

YOU spotted snakes with double tongue,
Thorny hedgehogs, be not seen;
Newts and blind-worms, do no wrong,
Come not near our fairy Queen!

Weaving spiders, come not here;
Hence, you long-legg'd spinners, hence!
Beetles black, approach not near;
Worm nor snail, do no offence.

Philomel, with melody
Sing in our sweet lullaby;
Lulla, lulla, lullaby, Lulla, lulla, lullaby:
Never harm
Nor spell nor charm
Come our lovely lady nigh:
So, Good Night, with lullaby.

WHEN daffodils begin to peer,
With heigh ! the doxy over the dale,
Why then comes in the sweet o' the year ;
For the red blood reigns in the winter's pale.

The white sheet bleaching on the hedge,
With heigh ! the sweet birds, O, how they sing !
Doth set my pugging tooth on edge ;
For a quart of ale is a dish for a king.

The lark, that tirra-lyra chants,
With heigh ! with heigh ! the thrush and the jay,
Are summer songs for me and my aunts,
While we lie tumbling in the hay.

But shall I go mourn for that, my dear?
  The pale moon shines by night:
And when I wander here and there,
  I then do most go right.

If tinkers may have leave to live
  And bear the sow-skin budget,
Then my account I well may give
  And in the stocks avouch it.

Jog on, jog on, the foot-path way,
  And merrily hent the stile-a:
A merry heart goes all the day,
  Your sad, tires in a mile-a.

LAWN as white as driven snow;
Cypress black as e'er was crow;
Gloves as sweet as damask roses;
Masks for faces and for noses;
Bugle bracelet, necklace amber,
Perfume for a lady's chamber;
Golden quoifs and stomachers,
For my lads to give their dears;
Pins and poking-sticks of steel,
What maids lack from head to heel:
Come buy of me, come; come buy, come buy;
Buy, lads, or else your lasses cry:
Come buy.

Will you buy any tape,
Or lace for your cape,
My dainty duck, my dear-a?
Any silk, any thread,
Any toys for your head,
Of the new'st and finest, finest wear-a?
Come to the pedlar;
Money's a medler
That doth utter all men's ware-a.

WHEN that I was and a little tiny boy,
With hey, ho, the wind and the rain,
A foolish thing was but a toy,
For the rain it raineth every day.

But when I came to man's estate,
'Gainst knaves and thieves men shut their gate.

But when I came, alas! to wive,
By swaggering could I never thrive.

But when I came unto my beds,
With toss-pots still had drunken heads.

A great while ago the world begun,
  With hey, ho, the wind and the rain,
But that's all one, our play is done,
  And we'll strive to please you every day.

WHEN daisies pied and violets blue
And lady-smocks all silver-white
And cuckoo-buds of yellow hue
Do paint the meadows with delight,
The cuckoo then, on every tree,
Mocks married men; for thus sings he,
Cuckoo;
Cuckoo, cuckoo:—O word of fear,
Unpleasing to a married ear!

When shepherds pipe on oaten straws
  And merry larks are ploughmen's clocks,
When turtles tread, and rooks, and daws,
  And maidens bleach their summer smocks,
The cuckoo then, on every tree,
Mocks married men ; for thus sings he,
            Cuckoo ;
Cuckoo, cuckoo :—O word of fear,
Unpleasing to a married ear !

O Mistress mine, where are you roaming?
O stay and hear; your true-love's coming
That can sing both high and low:
Trip no further, pretty sweeting;
Journeys end in lovers meeting,
Every wise man's son doth know.

What is Love? 'tis not hereafter;
Present mirth hath present laughter;
What's to come is still unsure:
In delay their lies no plenty;
Then come kiss me, sweet and-twenty:—
Youth's a stuff will not endure.

ART thou god, to shepherd turn'd,
That a maiden's heart hath burn'd?
Why, thy godhead laid apart,
Warr'st thou with a woman's heart?
Whiles the eye of man did woo me,
That could do no vengeance to me.
If the scorn of your bright eyne
Hath power to raise such love in mine,
Alack, in me what strange effect
Would they work in mild aspect!
Whiles you chid me, I did love;
How then might your prayers move!

He that brings this love to thee
Little knows this love in me:
And by him seal up thy mind;
Whether that thy youth and kind
Will the faithful offer take
Of me and all that I can make;
Or else by him my love deny,
And then I'll study how to die.

I

THEY bore him barefaced on the bier;
Hey non nonny, nonny, hey nonny;
And in his grave rain'd many a tear:—
You must sing a-down a-down,
An you call him a-down-a.

And will he not come again?
And will he not come again?
No, no, he is dead:
Go to thy death-bed:
He never will come again.

His beard was as white as snow,
All flaxen was his poll :
  He is gone, he is gone,
  And we cast away moan :
God ha' mercy on his soul !

II

Come o'er the bourn, Bessy, to me !
  —Her boat hath a leak,
  And she must not speak
Why she dares not come over to thee !

III

Sleepest or wakest thou, jolly shepherd?
  Thy sheep be in the corn;
And for one blast of thy minikin mouth,
  Thy sheep shall take no harm.

BLOW, blow, thou winter wind,
Thou art not so unkind
As man's ingratitude;
Thy tooth is not so keen,
Because thou art not seen,
Although thy breath be rude.
Heigh-ho! sing, heigh-ho! unto the green holly:
Most friendship is feigning, most loving mere folly:
Then, heigh-ho, the holly!
This life is most jolly.

Freeze, freeze, thou bitter sky,
That dost not bite so nigh
  As benefits forgot :
Though thou the waters warp,
Thy sting is not so sharp
  As friend remember'd not.
Heigh-ho ! sing, heigh-ho ! unto the green holly :
Most friendship is feigning, most loving mere folly :
Then, heigh-ho, the holly !
This is life most jolly.

UNDER the greenwood tree
Who loves to lie with me,
And tunes his merry note
Unto the sweet bird's throat,
Come hither, come hither, come hither!
Here shall he see
No enemy
But winter and rough weather.

Who doth ambition shun
And loves to live i' the sun,
Seeking the food he eats
And pleased with what he gets,
Come hither, come hither, come hither :
Here shall he see
No enemy
But winter and rough weather.

IMMORTAL gods, I crave no pelf;
I pray for no man but myself:
Grant I may never prove so fond,
To trust man on his oath or bond;
Or a harlot, for her weeping;
Or a dog, that seems a-sleeping;
Or a keeper with my freedom;
Or my friends, if I should need 'em.
Amen. So fall to't:
Rich men sin, and I eat root.

LOVE, Love, nothing but Love, still more!
For, O, love's bow
Shoots buck and doe:
The shaft confounds,
Not that it wounds,
But tickles still the sore.

These lovers cry Oh! oh! they die!
Yet that which seems the wound to kill,
Doth turn oh! oh! to ha! ha! he!
So dying love lives still:
Oh! oh! a while, but ha! ha! ha!
Oh! oh! groans out for ha! ha! ha!
—Heigh-ho!

WHEN icicles hang by the wall
And Dick the shepherd blows his nail
And Tom bears logs into the hall
And milk comes frozen home in pail,
When blood is nipp'd and ways be foul,
Then nightly sings the staring owl,
Tu-whit ;
Tu-who ;—a merry note ;—
While greasy Joan doth keel the pot.

When all aloud the wind doth blow
  And coughing drowns the parson's saw
And birds sit brooding in the snow
  And Marian's nose looks red and raw,
When roasted crabs hiss in the bowl,
Then nightly sings the staring owl,
        Tu-whit;
Tu-who;—a merry note;—
While greasy Joan doth keel the pot.

IF love make me forsworn, how shall I swear to
love?
Ah, never faith could hold, if not to beauty vow'd!
Though to myself forsworn, to thee I'll faithful
prove;
Those thoughts to me were oaks, to thee like osiers
bow'd.
Study his bias leaves and makes his book thine eyes,
Where all those pleasures live that art would
comprehend:
If knowledge be the mark, to know thee shall suffice;
Well learnéd is that tongue that well can thee
commend,

All ignorant that soul that sees thee without wonder;
Which is to me some praise that I thy parts admire:
Thy eye Jove's lightning bears, thy voice his dreadful thunder,
Which, not to anger bent, is music and sweet fire.
Celestial as thou art, O pardon, Love, this wrong,
That sings heaven's praise with such an earthly tongue!

THE master, the swabber, the boatswain and I,
The gunner and his mate,
Loved Mall, Meg and Marian and Margery,
But none of us cared for Kate;
For she had a tongue with a tang,
Would cry to a sailor, Go hang!
She loved not the savour of tar nor of pitch,
Yet a tailor might scratch her where'er she did itch:
Then to sea, boys, and let her go hang!

WHAT shall he have that kill'd the deer?
His leather skin and horns to wear.
Then sing him home;
Take thou no scorn to wear the horn;
It was a crest ere thou wast born:
Thy father's father wore it,
And thy father bore it!
The horn, the horn, the lusty horn
Is not a thing to laugh to scorn.

FULL fathom five thy father lies;
Of his bones are coral made;
Those are pearls that were his eyes:
Nothing of him that doth fade
But doth suffer a sea-change
Into something rich and strange.
Sea-nymphs hourly ring his knell:
Ding-dong.
Hark! now I hear them,—Ding-dong, bell.

P.W.

DO nothing but eat, and make good cheer,
And praise God for the merry year ;
When flesh is cheap and females dear,
And lusty lads roam here and there
So merrily,
And ever among so merrily.

Be merry, be merry, my wife has all ;
For women are shrews, both short and tall :
'Tis merry in hall when beards wag all,
And welcome merry Shrove-tide :—
Be merry, be merry !

A cup of wine that's brisk and fine,
And drink unto the leman mine;
    And a merry heart lives long-a.
Fill the cup, and let it come:
I'll pledge you a mile to the bottom.

COME, thou Monarch of the vine,
Plumpy Bacchus with pink eyne !
In thy vats our cares be drown'd,
With thy grapes our hairs be crown'd :
Cup us, till the world go round,
Cup us, till the world go round !

FATHERS that wear rags
Do make their children blind;
But fathers that bear bags
Shall see their children kind.
Fortune, that arrant whore,
Ne'er turns the key to the poor.

That sir, which serves and seeks for gain
And follows but for form,
Will pack when it begins to rain,
And leave thee in the storm.
But I will tarry; the fool will stay,
And let the wise man fly;
The knave turns fool that runs away;
The fool no knave, perdy.

TAKE, O, take those lips away
That so sweetly were forsworn;
And those eyes, the break of day,
Lights that do mislead the morn:
But my kisses bring again;
Seals of love, but seal'd in vain;
—Seal'd in vain.

HONOUR, riches, marriage-blessing,
Long continuance, and increasing,
Hourly joys be still upon you!
Juno sings her blessings on you.

Earth's increase, foison plenty,
Barns and garners never empty,
Vines with clustering bunches growing,
Plants with goodly burthen bowing;

Spring come to you at the farthest
In the very end of harvest!
Scarcity and want shall shun you;
Ceres' blessing so is on you.

THEN is there mirth in Heaven,
When earthly things made even
Atone together!
Good duke, receive thy daughter:
Hymen from heaven brought her,
Yea, brought her hither,
That thou mightest join her hand with his
Whose heart within his bosom is.

SONG

Wedding is great Juno's crown:
  O blessèd bond of board and bed!
'Tis Hymen peoples every town;
  High Wedlock then be honourèd:
Honour, high honour and renown,
To Hymen, god of every town!

ON a day—alack the day!—
Love, whose month is ever May,
Spied a blossom passing fair
Playing in the wanton air:
Through the velvet leaves the wind,
All unseen, 'gan passage find;
That the Lover, sick to death,
Wish himself the heaven's breath.
—Air, quoth he, thy cheeks may blow;
Air, would I might triumph so!
But, alack, my hand is sworn
Ne'er to pluck thee from thy thorn;

Vow, alack, for youth unmeet,
Youth so apt to pluck a sweet!
Do not call it sin in me,
That I am forsworn for thee;
Thou,—for whom Jove would swear
Juno but an Ethiope were,
And deny himself for Jove,
Turning mortal for thy love.

SO sweet a kiss the golden sun gives not
  To those fresh morning drops upon the rose,
As thy eye-beams, when their fresh rays have smote
  The night of dew that on my cheeks down flows:

Nor shines the silver moon one half so bright
  Through the transparent bosom of the deep,
As doth thy face through tears of mine give light;
  Thou shinest in every tear that I do weep:

No drop but as a coach doth carry thee;
  So ridest thou triumphing in my woe.
Do but behold the tears that swell in me,
  And they thy glory through my grief will show:

But do not love thyself; then thou wilt keep
My tears for glasses, and still make me weep.
O Queen of queens! how far dost thou excel,
No thought can think, nor tongue of mortal tell.

HOW should I your true-Love know
From another one?
By his cockle hat and staff,
And his sandal shoon.

He is dead and gone, lady,
He is dead and gone;
At his head a grass-green turf,
At his heels a stone.

White his shroud as the mountain snow,
Larded with sweet flowers;—
Which bewept to the grave did go
With true-love showers.

WAS this fair face the cause, quoth she
Why the Grecians sackéd Troy?
Fond done, done fond,
Was this King Priam's joy?

With that she sighéd as she stood,
With that she sighéd as she stood,
And gave this sentence then:
Among nine bad if one be good,
Among nine bad if one be good,
There's yet one good in ten.

HANG there, my verse, in witness of my love:
And thou, thrice-crownéd Queen of night, survey
With thy chaste eye, from thy pale sphere above,
The huntress' name that my full life doth sway.
O Rosalind! these trees shall be my books,
And in their barks my thoughts I'll character;
That every eye which in this forest looks
Shall see thy virtue witness'd every where.
Run, run, Orlando; carve on every tree
The fair, the chaste, and unexpressive She.

SWEET Mistress,—what your name is else, I know not,
Nor by what wonder you do hit of mine,—
Less in your knowledge and your grace you show not
Than our earth's wonder, more than earth, divine.
Teach me, dear creature, how to think and speak;
Lay open to my earthy-gross conceit,
Smother'd in errors, feeble, shallow, weak,
The folded meaning of your words' deceit.
Against my soul's pure truth why labour you
To make it wander in an unknown field?
Are you a god? would you create me new?
Transform me then, and to your power I'll yield!

IF She be made of white and red,
  Her faults will ne'er be known ;
For blushing cheeks by faults are bred
  And fears by pale white shown :
Then if she fear, or be to blame,
  By this you shall not know,—
For still her cheeks possess the same
  Which native she doth owe !

Autolycus—Dorcas—Mopsa

A. GET you hence, for I must go
Where it fits not you to know!
D. Whither? *M.* O whither? *D.* Whither?
M. It becomes thy oath full well
Thou to me thy secrets tell.
D. Me, too, let me go thither.
M. Or thou goest to the grange or mill.
D. If to either, thou dost ill.
A. Neither. *D.* What, neither? *A.* Neither.
D. Thou hast sworn my Love to be.
M. Thou hast sworn it more to me:
—Then whither goest? say, whither?

ORPHEUS with his lute made trees,
And the mountain tops that freeze,
Bow themselves when he did sing:
To his music plants and flowers
Ever sprung, as sun and showers
There had made a lasting spring.

Every thing that heard him play,
Even the billows of the sea,
Hung their heads, and then lay by.
In sweet music is such art,
Killing care and grief of heart
Fall asleep, or hearing, die.

TELL me where is Fancy bred,
Or in the heart or in the head?
How begot, how nourishéd?
—Reply, reply.
It is engender'd in the eyes,
With gazing fed; and Fancy dies
In the cradle where it lies.
Let us all ring Fancy's knell:
I'll begin it,—Ding, dong, bell:—
Ding, dong, bell.

HARK, hark! the lark at heaven's gate sings,
And Phœbus 'gins arise,
His steeds to water at those springs
On chaliced flowers that lies;
And winking mary-buds begin
To ope their golden eyes:
With every thing that pretty is.
My Lady sweet, arise:
Arise, arise!

Printed by BALLANTYNE, HANSON & Co.
London & Edinburgh

www.ingramcontent.com/pod-product-compliance
Lightning Source LLC
Chambersburg PA
CBHW030551270326
41927CB00008B/1597